LOVE AND ROMANCE

HOW CAN WE CREATE ROMANTIC ENVIRONMENT AND ATTRACT THE GIRLS WITH LOVE

"LOVE TO LOVE WITH LOVE IN LOVE"

S.N LEMAN

Contents

INTRODUCTION

"Because love is patient; love is generous; he is not jealous. He was not boastful and not arrogant. He didn't do anything rude and didn't seek his own advantage. He is not hot-tempered and does not hold onto the faults of others. True and pure love, unconditional love."

CHAPTER 1

LOVE ITU FUN!!

Not all of our grandmothers and grandfathers know and have experience with dating, unlike today's modern youth. It is said that the story used to be that the prospective grandmother or grandfather had been prepared since they were little. This means that since childhood there has been a partner to be a wife or husband, there is no chance to be picky anymore. Well, what the couple will make can be the children of friends, relatives or other people who have been ordered or "bought" since childhood. But today is certainly different, we live in an era that should be for things to find a partner, parents are expected not to interfere in matters. You want to hunt yourself, track and survey yourself, and if necessary, parents just accept that it's done, and most importantly don't embarrass parents and people in the village. Don't let it happen the NBA, not that famous

Basketball club, People say that courtship is a continuation of acquaintance and then continued with young people's relationships with the opposite sex. (Oh yes, this article is specifically about dating the opposite sex, yes, because in this crazy era, there are people who date the samc kind). So in this courtship, boys and girls explore each other how compatible and bickering they are, including background, character, character, nature, education, hobbies and others. This relationship is more than just a friend (friend) or friend close, but these are the closest and closest of friends, trying to understand one another.

Maturity of dating, depending on the behavior of the one who is dating, sometimes we still find various rah-rah in dating, so dating is identified with watching, eating together, showing off, then proclaiming this, my boyfriend, who is your girlfriend? (Beautiful? Handsome?). Even though dating is a continuation of our acquaintance, it means that we have advanced one more step. People who are dating should be at the serious stage of thinking about their future, no longer like children or being reckless. Therefore, in the opportunities that exist during courtship, we need to fill it as well as possible to find out and get to know our partner more closely, so that later when we get married, we already know him and don't regret it for the rest of our lives. Rice when it becomes porridge, how long a person has been dating depends on the two people, there are people who meet for a month or two and are really desperate, half a year later asking for marriage. But there are those who have been dating for 10 years and are still unmarried (until they get bored?). But it's a shame if you haven't been married for 10 years, it could be talk and gossip from your neighbor's right - left. The community is evil, the words are very piercing and heart-wrenching "Dating took, when are you getting married?"

The ancients said love is "from the eyes down to the heart", that's why it takes time to detect, when the first sight used is the eye, so start looking here and there, glancing, even glaring to see clearly which one is suitable, After that, a period of acquaintance and courtship is also needed by the heart, in order to feel the deepest love.

I have a friend, when he was dating, people knew the girls didn't really agree, the reason being the guy didn't have one, his school wasn't finished yet, his work wasn't stable either. Long story short, a girl's parents strictly forbid dating. But the basis is already desperate to fall in love, so the prohibition of parents is violated and ignored, but the positive is the guy struggles and keeps on fighting. He knows that if he is considered less bona fide, there is no title and money, car, house or anything else. That's why the guy is actively studying while working, one or two years later he opened his own business.

In the third year the boy has been successful, this time his parents really salute the boy's struggle. The courtship permit came out, amazing! Now these are positive things, young people need to emulate, he is not just joking and reckless, there is a desperate struggle, and his love is pure and not kidding. The bad thing is when the guy is secretly invites elopement, that's called a shortcut. As a result, what happens? Quickly have children, no title, still work as a "lawyer", namely unemployment with many events.

I really agree that people who are dating are already "adults", at least they can earn money. Don't want to invite the girl to watch it still ask her parents, then it's a hassle! Well, if the guy hasn't worked yet, then their courtship will be too long, because every time he is asked when he wants to get married, the answer is always not ready. Waiting for college, finished college, still waiting for a job, already got a job waiting to collect money first, then when you have a lot of money, strange behavior begins to appear. Looking for another girlfriend too? How are you?? Unless the parents are rich, it doesn't matter, there is or no work, the parents will sponsor the marriage, and even a nice house has been provided. But it should be the girl, need to think twice or three if you get a guy who usually relies on his parents? Until when?? Nitra is like a bird in a cage, the cage is good, but the occupants don't feel free.

Dating also has its dangers, you know? Adults should already know! Why do I say that! When the girl and boy sit together, close together again, Wong is a normal human being; there's a stun. Now if the stun is not controlled, there is a danger, that's why you need to be vigilant, I'm sure you understand the point. In the Western world, those who are dating, kissing and kissing are not something that needs to be censored, on red light streets, in parking lots, even in Super Markets, which makes people resentful that someone dares to be in front of us, isn't it crazy? That's called sneezing! Moreover, his style is carried away by lust. Can be "dangerous ... Kate people from Jakarta"

How to find a girlfriend and where is it? This question is quite interesting to answer, because some people say that looking for a girlfriend should be on campus, especially where there are many campus flowers that are perched, especially in the cafeteria or library. Someone said that there is also the office where we work, in the church too? Others said that in bookstores, recently there are certain bookstores that can be a place for men or women to visit, usually those who go there don't buy or read books, just look around, while washing their eyes; who knows acquaintances and can date there. Well, this is additional motivation from someone, besides studying, working or worshiping, and visiting a bookstore, there is "Shrimp behind the stone". Poor bookstore!!

Nowadays, you can also find a girlfriend at the War net (Internet Cafe), how come? Yes, you can, through chatting with people, but the danger is that many people like to lie about their status. Even so, there are couples I know who are married and the way to get to know them is through the Internet, now they are married and living abroad. There are others who are currently dating, young people say.

For sure don't look for girlfriends in night clubs, or places for drunken people, and ecstasy, you will get additional work, besides your parents disagree, friends too, except your friends all residents there.

Oh yes, below is an excerpt that I have revised in such a way, some tips for finding a boyfriend interspersed with gossip. Want to try?

First: Look for a boyfriend that suits your situation, don't be like back missing the moon, and just look for it according to your standards. For example, if you want to be a wife who is an economist, then you must also study at the Faculty of Economics, so that when you are in college you don't even graduate, at least you will meet a husband who is an economist.

Second: Look for a handsome and beautiful girlfriend and don't look for an ugly one, but usually the ugly one will become beautiful when you fall in love, you must also be kind. The reason is, handsome and beautiful can't be bought, indeed from there (read soon), and it won't hurt to get a handsome one, but you need to be careful everything that looks outside is not a guarantee, handsomeness and beauty will soon pass with time, even those who handsome and beautiful more easily snatched by others. A person's behavior can change 180 degrees, as long as he wants to repent. That's if you can find someone who is brave, but fears God. A handsome and beautiful girlfriend will also improve offspring in the future, once again this is only an estimate, not a guarantee!

Third: Find a girlfriend who is rich and works hard, because the material is necessary too! Yes, not 100%, because if you have a boyfriend who is broke and lazy, even though he is as handsome as the F-4 star Tao Ming Se and you will be miserable because your wealth will soon run out, you have to help find money and work hard. However, on the other hand, if he is really working hard, there is no need to worry.

Fourth: You have a mirror in your house, if you don't have a pretty face, you know a little bit about choosing a boyfriend. Do not set the target too high, it will not be achieved. But beyond your expectations and you will be surprised, people who do not belong to the category of college flowers, sometimes get a handsome husband too.

Fifth: Don't love your boyfriend so much that he forgets everything, let alone forgets God, forgets his studies in college, forgets his job and forgets himself. Currently you are just dating, what if you are married, really don't remember everything. If in the middle of a courtship there is a problem and they break up, your mother will find it very difficult; hang yourself on a chili tree.

Sixth: There is a suggestion that if the stock of Indonesian production runs out, just look for a girlfriend who is Caucasian, it is said that the story is that Caucasians are tall, handsome and handsome, as long as they don't look for unemployed ones. The citizens are also overseas again, cool, you will be brought there.

Excuse me asking, do you have a boyfriend? Have you thought about the seriousness of living together in the future? Guaranteed you will not be banned by your parents if you are an adult. Because if it is forbidden for you to go on a date, then they can go crazy. So be single. At this time, what is important when dating is to be responsible and not play games? Dating is not a sin, as long as it is on the path of etiquette, moral values, ethics and decency. The most important thing is not to play with your girlfriend, because "the boyfriend" is not a toy, even though there are people who like to play with him. Strong lol.

CHAPTER 2

HOWA PARTYN YANG REASONABLE?

The courtship will definitely bring good or bad things, meaning that if the courtship is carried out according to the rules, then it doesn't mess around, which means it doesn't violate the path set by God, then most will run it happily. On the other hand, if the courtship is carried out as I wish, and then does not fear God, then do not expect good results.

In the free world, especially in our country which has been independent for 60 years, you are free to date, but free in the sense that it is not arbitrary. Still there are limits, there are limits to ethics, morals, and manners. If you dare to violate it, then the risk will be borne by yourself.

So now what is meant by proper dating?

The number of girlfriends is one

What is natural, of course, is that someone is dating one person, so there is no such thing as a spare tire. Dating will be unnatural if the boy or girl has the intention at the same time to date more from one person. Friends, ordinary friends may have more than one and as many as possible, but the one chosen to be a girlfriend must be one; unless it doesn't match, then separate and find another girlfriend.

Not binding

Dating is different from marriage, so it's still not binding, so it's very natural that those who are dating if they still have a lot of friends, the problem is that it's not binding. If you are still dating, you are already bound like "imprisoned", you can't imagine if you are married.

About a dozen years ago when I was still a teacher, there was a female coworker of mine, whose boyfriend was very jealous. It happened because his girlfriend couldn't pick him up that day, then another Physics teacher took him to the bus station, so there was a problem the next day. The guy came looking for her, and a fight broke out, what a shame.

Mature

In terms of dating, maturity is also needed, we have already mentioned before that dating which is just having fun, eating, traveling, seems to be a waste of money and time. No time to get to know each other. Everyone is unique, the background is different, and the nature and way of teaching from parents is also different. All these differences will be tried to unite in an unknown but short period of time. There are people who have only been dating for half a year and are married, some are more than that. It is estimated that there is not enough time to get to know each other more deeply, therefore dating is an opportunity that exists for our maturity to get to know one another. Differences of opinion and the concept is possible, but mature brands have an attitude of respect and respect for the opinions of others.

Balanced

Balanced in a broad sense, economy, education, age and faith. Too many problems are found if they are dating and don't pay attention to this balance. Indeed not all, but generally, those from rich families will underestimate the poor, those who are educated will feel superior. Likewise with age, it is quite surprising if we see that there are couples whose age difference is striking. Some couples have a relationship with full loyalty, but not infrequently they live it with various motivations, some are because of seeing wealth so that the girl is willing to marry the gray one, even though the handsome and young are waiting a lot.

Love

Mutual love is the main key in normal dating. Love is also not in the sense of feeling sorry for our girlfriend. But the love that springs from the depths of the heart, which begins with first sight, is then continued by getting to know one another. A normal courtship should involve mutual love, because this is an important foundation. Without love, the name is not dating, it's just a friend or best friend.

Patience & self-control

Love produces patience, and proper courtship also requires patience, it should not precede it if it is not yet time. Those who are dating must restrain themselves, must not violate the territory and boundaries of ethics and morals, especially in close relationships. Dating is not a standard die to marry, that's why if one day it doesn't match, then when the two people make the decision to separate, then the separation is also a good farewell, meaning that they do not become enemies, but there is a change from special friends to ordinary friends.

Now I want to ask you who are dating. Is your courtship in a reasonable position? Or is it unnatural so that it crosses forbidden boundaries. An unnatural courtship will harm both parties, both male and female, because it gives the impression that they do not respect each other. Come back to reasonable limits!!

CHAPTER 3

LOVE A IT UBLIND, ORANG G BUT A BER LOVE

Is it true that love is blind? If love is blind, how come blind people can make love too? Oh yes, what is certain is that love can make us blind. Why is that? Does love have poison? There's no poison, yes, but the effect is, wow is it perishable? People who are desperate to fall in love, can change completely, just imagine, suddenly that person can be very diligent, usually wakes up in the morning at 12.00 noon, once falling in love waking up can be a clock 6:00 morning, because that morning he would take his lover to campus. If it's usually just a light drizzle, you won't want to be invited outside, now even a snowstorm is still going to pick up your lover. The impact is huge! Now again, for positive things, it doesn't matter if they are transmitted, as long as it's not negative. On the other hand, if it's because of love, you are lazy to study, spree, then this is something that needs to be questioned? But the possibility exists, so you need to be careful.

There are people who are really "blind" because of love, then here and there people accuse him of being subject to witchcraft or witchcraft, even though basically he is desperate to fall in love. That love made him not eat and drink all day without feeling hungry. I didn't see each other for a day, it felt like a year. Love is blind, when we see someone who suddenly falls in love with people we don't expect at all, for example in a big-time criminal, a drunk, gambler or ecstasy drinker, or a woman of the night. Maybe people are surprised, why does he still want to be with people like that? But the basis of love, love is blind.

People who have fallen in love are sometimes desperate, and don't care about their parents or the advice of the priest, the important thing is that if they are in love, they move forward like soldiers, even if they don't get their approval, it's okay. To this day, there are still many couples who are forced to separate, due to pressure and pressure and threats from their parents, but not a few are desperate, they take shortcuts, namely elopement (meaning not while running, but without parental consent). So, as a result, he was embarrassed, he himself was embarrassed, his parents were also embarrassed; but what matters to them both is love. If that's the case, parents don't want it or not, because what else do they want to say? It's just a pity for the child, once again society is evil, I've heard of a schoolboy who was teased by his neighbors' children that he was born because his parents eloped? "Oh yes your Papa and Mama eloped", I don't know who taught them to say that? Maybe his parents will tell.

Actually love itself is not blind, the proof is that he is still able to distinguish which one is the lover and which one is not consciously, which is beautiful and which is ugly, for sure people who have fallen in love don't care who they love. The girl who is generally judged by people to be less beautiful, but her personal judgment can change to be beautiful like an angel descending from heaven. On the other hand, the less handsome guy seemed to him like Silvester Stallone who had just come out of Hollywood.

It is said that in a village there lived an ugly woman. So bad that young people stay away from it. There is a custom in the village to give a dowry to a man who wants to propose to the girl of his dreams, the amount of dowry given depends on the beauty of the girl. So if the girl has an ordinary face, then her dowry is worth a goat. If it's more beautiful, the number of goats will increase. And the highest dowry until then was the prima donna dowry in the village, as many as 10 goats.

Everyone was talking about the 'price' of that ugly girl. They said: "Ah, he's ugly. No one wants it. Let alone a goat, there's definitely no chicken." And another said: "Never mind a chicken, no one wants to pay for it with a dead chicken carcass.' And they laughed at the fate of the poor girl.

The girl heard their jokes over and over again, and her heart became sad and hurt. Her pride was damaged, and she herself almost believed, that no one would take her as a wife. Until one day, word got out that the ugly girl was being edited by a young man from the other side of the village. And the villagers wondered, which poor young man was "blind" to propose to the ugly girl? They flocked to the house of the ugly girl's parents and intended to inquire about the truth of this matter. And to their surprise, when they got there, they found the young man's dowry. The dowry is a cow! No beautiful woman has ever been given such an expensive and precious dowry! Even the prettiest girl in the village was only 'worth' 10 goats.

They became more curious. Therefore, the people flocked to the other side of the village to see how the ugly woman was. Millions of questions arise, maybe the young man is crazy? His eyes are blind, don't you see if he's ugly half to death?"

"Ah, maybe they're just used as housemaids, they must be given a little food and then sold back to the slave traders." When they arrived at the young man's house, they saw that the house was very luxurious. The walls are beautifully carved. And they were increasingly convinced that their suspicions about this poor woman being made a housemaid and a slave were not wrong.

When they knocked on the door, a handsome young man greeted them. He introduced himself as the owner of the house. They asked if they could meet the girl. The young man returned to the house, after inviting them to sit in the living room. A beautiful young woman came to greet them. His hair was neatly arranged, his speech was smooth and soft, and he kindly invited them to take food and drink. The people asked, where is the ugly girl? Are you okay? Where is he now? The beautiful woman replied, "I am the one". The people stared, stared, and were unable to speak. They ask? Is it true? Isn't it wrong to see? That girl is so ugly, while this woman is very graceful and beautiful?

The woman said, "I feel beautiful, when I know that my husband values me at a great price. I realize that he is not just trying to say that I am beautiful, not what people say, more so because he loves me. In return, I try to give the best that I can ever give, because I know my husband paid a very high price for me, I dress beautifully, I change my hairstyle, and try to please her. And this is who I am now." This story is just a child's fairy tale, but the message is clear, love can make you more beautiful, if you don't believe it, please try it?

Blind love has produced illogical thinking, no sense at all. When the world and everyone around says it's not good, those who fall in love say it's very good.

When the world admits that a person is not beautiful, those who fall in love say that they are very beautiful. This blind love has caused a person to be willing to sacrifice himself. Once there was a young couple secretly making love, but their parents did not agree. Besides the guy being a few years easier than the girl, the guy is also still in college, the story is not independent. The girl's parents tried to separate her daughter from the boy, finally she tried to send her daughter to study abroad. But what happened, the night before she left abroad, she left the house with the guy, and disappeared for almost a week. Where are they hiding? His cellular wasn't activated, and he didn't tell anyone? The boy's family also did not know anything about his son's departure, the story is that the parents of both parties are looking for each other.

Because of this panic and confusion, the couple's parents finally met somewhere, uh, it turns out that these two parents already know each other, they were friends in elementary school.

The story is just like a movie. I'm sure you'll know the end of this story? The sixth day they returned home, after there was a guarantee from their respective parents that they would not be separated again? Well luckily they are still "aware" that they are still hiding in the house of a distant relative, try if they are in a hotel or forbidden places, they will soon be married without a party! I hope this is not an example for you? Love is blind, at the same time makes desperate!!

CHAPTER 4

CHOOSE A GIRLFRIEND THAT BEAUTIFUL DONG!!!

Beautiful face, who doesn't like it! You and I will definitely like it. Our friends like it too, don't they? Starting from small children, teenagers, youth to adults, even eng kong - eng kong and mothers love beauty. That's why it's not surprising, many women don't hesitate to spend their money just taking care of beauty problems. He is willing to force himself on a diet so that his body is slim and beautiful to look at, fasts for days it doesn't matter, the important thing is that the money can be saved to pay for his care. Most, most and most importantly she will look beautiful. With this beautiful capital, he will attract the attention of many people, because everyone likes the beautiful.

What is beauty really for? Wow, beauty is apparently to be seen and seen by other people besides ourselves, sometimes because of this beauty problem our mirror can become a victim just because someone's face appears an uninvited pimple, this happens because he doesn't can resist the taste of fried peanuts. Then he started to smear himself with various spices eh wrong with a variety of powders in order to quickly get rid of the naughty pimples that are on his face.

Recently I was sent an email containing the faces of beautiful artists when they were not preening and then their faces were also included when they were prepped, well it turns out that they are uglier than women who are generally seen by the human eye as ugly. In other words, it turns out that her beauty is just a mere polish, or a rough trick of human vision. I think if there is a chance, we can organize a beauty pageant for women without preening. Well, at that time it will be known who is truly original, who is actually the most naturally and naturally beautiful or the "chemically beautiful" one, meaning that it is polished with chemicals in the form of expensive powders and lipsticks and markers.

One day there was a husband who was a little annoyed with his wife. Because he likes to preen and choose clothes for hours every time he wants to travel. Moreover, coupled with every outfit that is tried on, the husband is always asked, "Isn't it beautiful yet?" While the husband has answered "yes, it's beautiful", but the wife is still not satisfied, then replaces it with something else. Suddenly after repeatedly changing clothes again, the husband asked, "Isn't it enough that I told you were beautiful"? Who else do you want to show off to? Do you still expect other people to be interested in you? Beauty is not unnecessary actually, don't want to travel and just do it without preening, it will embarrass your husband.

In our real world, beauty plays a very important role, for example, when managers recruit secretaries, they must choose a beautiful face. To show off luxury cars, beautiful women are displayed in sexy clothes, then artists are also in general who are beautiful, men choose a boyfriend, must also choose a beautiful one, although in fact beauty is very subjective and relative, but according to the standard of a man's glasses his future wife must be the most beautiful in the world. It is said that once upon a time there was only one most beautiful woman in the world, namely Eve, because at that time there was no rival. If now there are so many women so that there are quite a lot of rivals.

Actually love and the size of a person's ideal partner is not a matter of beauty or not, look at the mothers and eng kong-eng kong they are still faithful hand in hand going everywhere, sometimes hugging, still close and love each other. If beauty is their standard, they must have separated a long time ago, because now they are TOP aka Old, Toothless and Potted. The question is, why is that? The answer is because it is not beauty that is a measure, but there is something beyond that beauty, which is in the deepest heart, the inner beauty, the hidden inner beauty.

There are people who say that, do not love because of beauty, but it is precisely because we love that she becomes beautiful. So it's not surprising that we often find women with beautiful faces, most of their partners are beyond our calculations, meaning they are not as handsome as we think are commensurate, I say "mostly" which means certainly not absolute. The couple in question is also not because of "marriage" with the motivation of wealth, because it happened in my hometown there was a businessman who was rich but was old, but remarried with a wife who was only in her twenties.

Beauty is not important in matters of love. But that doesn't mean women don't need to preen, so they appear as they are and let their fat bodies sag. If this happens, the world will not be as beautiful as it is today, although in fact beauty is a lot of lies.

Now excuse me, if beauty is not that important, then what is important? Frankly speaking, what does it mean for a woman to be beautiful, beautiful and charming, but her life is chaotic, has a bad heart, likes to get drunk, is addicted to drugs, is a heavy smoker, likes to talk dirty, wears clothes that are fun and so on. God's Word says "like a gold earring on a pig's ledge, so is a beautiful woman who is not immoral." The sight of a woman who looks like this makes the standards of these beautiful women sink and become cheap. Not to mention coupled with the beautiful women who usually have many male friends, most likely also many girlfriends. Now if that happens, then the standard will drop even more, he is like a trophy that keeps changing owners, Monday night Charlie's girlfriend, Tuesday night Budi appears, There is one beauty that cannot be bought and cannot be lost, namely the beauty from within which, as I mentioned above, is inner beauty. Although we do not explore deep into what inner beauty is, but we can see that the beauty that is within is above all else. That is why in the Song of Solomon, King Solomon writes about his black but beautiful maiden (Song of Solomon 1:5), a judgment that really comes from the bottom of the heart, not based on general standards. Usually when he is black, he is embarrassed to say that he is beautiful, but this black man is so confident in saying that he is indeed beautiful. He truly values himself as a noble creation. That's why in Indonesia we often hear the word Hitam Manis, we rarely hear Sweet White, so when it's white it means danger, that's why white is called pale. It's no wonder so many white people like to sunbathe on the beach, to make it look a little black.

The beauty that is in a person is more meaningful than the beauty on the face. We have already explained that beauty because of the face can cause various problems of lies, which are very dependent on beauty tools, besides being temporary. But inner beauty is not like that, it is imprinted in the person and never fades. Concretely, what is the meaning of a girl who is beautiful in face, but is impudent, disrespectful, likes to hold grudges, is rude, never forgives others, is not easy-going but works only with preening, does not feel at home, likes to insult others, always fights with her friends even arrogant with her beauty?

A person who is beautiful before God is someone who understands that beauty is a gift from God, and that money cannot be bought. That's why no one is arrogant. Not necessarily that a beautiful person ends up getting a handsome husband, who is rich, and all the best, but often because of his arrogance over his beauty, he has to be shunned by many people, friends are also few or even non-existent. Not a few I found there were women who were beautiful when they were easy, many even had a crush on them, but because they were expensive and arrogant, in the end she had to live alone.

Besides that, people whose lives are beautiful in front of God will definitely love others, forgiveness will be very easy to give. For those who have pure love in themselves, surely they will also be loved by others. But if other people hate him, there must be something wrong. It is very beautiful, of course, beautiful people also love God, and so there is a special balance. Thus, they are born who are beautiful from within, beautiful in personality, beautiful character and spiritual beauty, while the beauty on the face has become very relative. Well, such a person is really beautiful, isn't it?

Now excuse me, which one do you want to choose, polished beauty or inner beauty? What is polished will soon be lost, the inner is always there. God loves us, he doesn't put beauty requirements on us. This means that God accepts us as we are, His only demand is one, total surrender to Him, that's all. Then if you choose a girlfriend, how? Then in unison the voices of the youths cheered "Choose a pretty girlfriend, right?" Okay, please choose the beautiful one, especially the beautiful inside and out.

CHAPTER 5

FALL IN LOVE

"Falling in love, a million tastes", Wow. ... This is a sentence I heard when I was a teenager, when the song by the beautiful grandmother Titik Puspa was sung by Mr. Eddy Silitonga entered a row of hits on the Indonesian popular songs chart. At this time, I don't know much about the popular love songs circulating in Indonesia, but I'm sure there are many songs that were created with the flavor of love.

In general, everyone is very impressed with the thing called love, some very famous films from ancient times until now in Indonesia, starting with Romeo and Juliet, Endless Love, Titanic, Sam Pek Eng Tai, then a series of other films by Gita Sinta from high school, "Meteor garden" with F-4, and the last one is the national film "What's with love?", not to mention the telenovela, all of which were released plus the national film against which the Circulation protested: "Hurry to kiss Gue Don?". Then there are also movie stars who are known for acting in love films, there is Rano Carno who is set with Jesse Guzman or Lydia Kandau, and for Hong Kong films there is Teng Kuang Yung and Liem Chin Shia and so on. Meanwhile, the public ranges from wealthy people to rickshaw brothers, from non-schoolers to scientists. Why is this? Because love is very beautiful, very interesting and amazing. Love can generate laughter and tears.

When we talk about love, it causes different impressions for those who hear it, depending on how each perceives love itself. Some caught him with a sullen face, some blushed, some blushed, and some even smiled happily. There are others who pretend not to know, who are ashamed but desire, and some who are angry. The last one for those who are angry may feel disappointed in love. Love can make people eat a glass of ice cream together, but love can also make people drink Baigon together.

Meanwhile, the distance between love and hate is neighbors, even the few who make love break their commitments, turn into hatred. Maybe at first it was like the title of a fifteen year old popular song "Hate But Rindu" sung by Diana Nasution, then if it doesn't last longer it will turn into "Goodbye Darling" sung by Noor Afni Octavia, and finally in a song an offer appears. That song that says "Too late you came to me"? Love can produce a sentence in which you are not sorry!

Love makes people angry, clumsy, changes their lives, makes them dapper, or turns them completely 180 degrees. A singer named Gomblo once said that love makes Cat Dung Taste Brown, but I'm not sure, if you want to try it, I don't forbid it.

Now we ask, what exactly is love?

You still remember rhymes like this right? Where do leeches come from? From the fields down to the river. Where does love come from? From the eyes to the heart. So love is said from the eyes down to one's heart. But maybe you want to protest, because it turns out that even blind people can make love, so what else is there to do? Is the poem wrong? Or how!

Let's ask again the meaning of love? Love is an expression of the deepest feelings of affection and cannot be realized by an item or anything, love concerns our feelings for someone or an object, but usually love is synonymous with affection between the opposite sex, for example boys to girls or vice versa.

In this crazy era, it turns out that those who are boys with boys or vice versa can make love. There are even churches in America that have recognized gay and lesbian marriage, the world is getting crazy!! God's word is twisted. That's why a mother once said, be grateful, if your child understands dating, then he understands how to choose a partner of the opposite sex.

Love starts from love which then continues to grow and form imperceptibly, even becoming very attached to one another with a form of affection, so that those who are already captivated do not easily erase the love from their hearts. If the person is not ready, then a breakup can result in disastrous consequences, such as mental illness and even suicide. There are also those who have been disappointed in love, they decide to live a celibate life or be alone, not wanting to make love again.

The word love (love) is a word that has many meanings, you will be confused yourself when trying to define it according to the love dictionary you read. For example, someone says we love our hearts, but we also love Bakmi or Orange Juice. In other words, are we comparing our lover to Noodles or Orange Juice? Not really! That's why it's confusing isn't it??

How does it feel to be in love?

Is this question interesting enough

to listen to? People who fall in love feel everything blooms, sometimes smile to themselves, then start combing hair repeatedly, girls whose bodies are fertile trying to reduce until it reaches a standard weight, he is willing to leave delicious food, even though yesterday before falling in love, he ate that food. Starting from chocolate, McDonald's and Kentucky Fried Chicken, but now the food is vegetarian, the drink has turned into bitter tea.

It's also interesting if you've watched just one Indian film, usually in addition to presenting a fight scene there is also a love scene. I don't know why in Indian movies, people who make love are always running and hiding under the trees. While singing hand in hand, this is a hallmark of Indians. It's different if Westerners make love, the toys are in the room, now this is more troublesome and often crosses territorial boundaries.

There is a writer who often writes in newspapers saying that falling in love can make people stupid? Wow... interesting too? Why be stupid? I'm trying to understand what that means? Thinks have thoughts, it's true, people who fall in love can be like fools. Sometimes he smiles to himself, laughs to himself, sometimes talks to himself, sometimes looks at the mirror for a long time while going back and forth like a fashion show, but sometimes he cries alone, sometimes screams, sometimes gets angry. It's weird isn't it? Thankfully, this is still a normal limit, but there are things that are even worse, sometimes going to places far away and alone, then trying to jump into the river, trying to hang yourself (if the cayenne pepper tree is okay, but if you choose the Kedondong tree, it can be troublesome, very dangerous) and once happened someone drank mosquito repellent in the bathroom of a restaurant, luckily the person was saved; but it is enough to disturb and trouble many people. This is what it feels like to be in love.

So it's true that love has a million

tastes, millions are enough, and if it's billions it will feel very dizzy? Because millions of it feels dizzy enough! How? Are you still dizzy? If you are confused, you will definitely fall in love again, oh fall in love, it feels like a million!!

CHAPTER 6

NINE CHARACTERISTICS OF ONE COWOK JAOH LOVE

It can be seen that if our younger siblings are still small, they will not feel ashamed if they are asked to join hands between a boy and a girl. Sometimes also play hugs and kisses. Well, starting from our teenage years, there was a time when we saw boys and girls as enemies. Well why else then? Especially if at school, they are like Dogs with Cats. However, when the age of youth rises, there is a total change, at that time he begins to be interested in the opposite sex, so it is not surprising that he wants to be close to the opposite sex. Sticks like postage stamps, oh yeah now stamps aren't selling so well, have they been since email?

Now the problem is whether there are signs or gestures that can be smelled when someone falls into what is called falling in love? Oh of course there is! The nature of falling in love is like a negative like a 'carcass' that we can't hide, one day we will find out. As the saying goes, as clever as a squirrel jumps, it eventually falls to the ground, meaning that the secret must be revealed if someone is dating, because his behavior is strange and special. Below I try to give 9 characteristics of a guy who is in love:

Pretending to be shy

As reckless and as bad as a person is and how brave a person is if he "falls in love" he will surely turn out to be a good person. Usually the ones whose voices are loud when they speak are now very soft. Usually likes to talk dirty, so now he seems very polite. After that he was shy towards the person, sometimes pretending to do something to get attention. He is shy but willing, this is what is called a shy cat.

Like Glancing

Glancing is normal for those who are

interested, sometimes they don't dare to openly glance at them, and so they look at them stealthily. The funny thing is that when the person who glances at him turns his head, the person who looks at him pretends not to see him. It is said that someone said, a day without glancing at the person feels like a year, this time he was reluctant, but willing. Believe it or not, the first glance is "unforgettable", that's why if the girl and the boy also glance at each other, their eyes meet, wow what a joy!!! Couldn't sleep that night, not because there were lots of mosquitoes or drinking coffee, but because I fell in love.

Can't eat and sleep

People who fall in love feel like a day without seeing each other is like a year. So sometimes due to falling in lovc, you can't eat and don't sleep. His heart was always beating fast, not a heartache but a constant thought. Moreover, today there are sentences that touch the feeling, it will stay up late who is drunk in love. You don't feel hungry, especially when you're already talking on the phone, can't remember the time anymore, didn't sleep well, he kept dreaming.

Keep daydreaming

Daydreaming feels like a subscription for people who fall in love, sometimes the movie they watch is likened to him as the main character. Sad songs about love will also be consumption for those who are in love. To spark his heart, then he plays the love songs, as if the song represents him to talk to loved ones. Sometimes love can make the person's work neglected, because his mind begins to branch.

Touch

The touch in question is not touching, because it's just the stage of starting a courtship, still approaching (PDKT) so it's still uncomfortable to bump into dengue singers, don't know if you'll end up being embarrassed. The touch through the handshake for a long time is enough to stun love, wow amazing.

I want to meet you

A day without seeing each other has been almost a year, so I want every day, every hour, and every second to meet. That's why those who are dating long distances are a bit troublesome, apart from not meeting each other, communication is a bit difficult. Fortunately, there is now the Internet, so e-mail is very effective, coupled with chatting via Messenger, you can see your girlfriend's face via Web Cam and talk to her right away. Cheap!! But it's still different, yes, by meeting directly, but yes, its okay, rather than nothing. What are you waiting for??

Talking endlessly

I don't know what is being said, basically people who are dating can talk for hours, until the phone is hot. In addition, their telephone accounts have also swelled, especially for those who have to use long distance means. Once again, now the internet network can be used to chat. The story material may be from infancy to adulthood, then repeated again, not endlessly. There's a lot of lies, uh, there's a lot of wrong stories.

Helpful

I used to always wake up late, but once we were dating wow, it changed 180 degrees, he can get up early. It even looks lighter (diligent), so there are good looks, and positive changes. Diligent, of course, specifically aimed at the girlfriend, if it's the same as others, it's the same!! Unfortunately, it still doesn't seem to have changed.

Neat appearance

Combs and hair oil and perfume are not left behind. Previously, it was enough to wear T-shirts without ironing them, shorts and flip-flops, now they are starting to wear neat clothes, decent pants and branded shoes. Yesterday he was just any man, now he is no ordinary man.

CHAPTER 7

TENH KHABITS JELEK ORANG Dating

Why is it called a bad habit of dating people anyway? Are there no more good habits? There is, only this one is special, we highlight the bad. It should be more than 10, but because of the time and size of the book, we only give 10:

Origin of Sorbet

Seeing that all of my friends already have boyfriends, they start like worms that are hit by ashes, can't calm down, and haven't finished yet. Moreover, age is getting older, so what can you do? Now it's okay with boys, it's not a problem for girls, sometimes the parents seem "evil" like that, he keeps pressing his son to have a girlfriend; but how come no one has a crush yet, if it doesn't match, it's a different story, meaning that there are many who have a crush but no one has been chosen yet, the problem is why it's quiet, silent in a thousand languages, in the world there don't seem to be any more boys. Or conversely, the old man used to be picky, so that made the boys back off one by one, now people are getting lazy again. That's why, now, it's up to you, as long as someone tries it, they want it right away, now this is of course the name from Sorbet,

Love dimly lit places

Dating is often identified with dimness, it is said to be safe and romantic, even though in that place there are many mosquitoes and temptations. But people who are already busy dating, will not remember the mosquito bites, even though when they want to sleep, there is only one mosquito, the irritation is not playing. And surprisingly the dimly lit place is usually quiet and for people who are dating there is the best place, there are no distractions. But be careful, yes, humans don't bother, but there are demons, you know. What is certain is that you want to go to a quiet place, sometimes there are those who choose to go to the cemetery, so at that time be careful with the fireflies, there's nothing wrong, it's just that, sometimes it gives you goosebumps too. Concrete examples of many dating couples who died on the beach in Ancol in a position of dating. All this for wanting a quiet place, alone, finally.... Isn't it scary huh?

Sticks like a stamp

The bad habit of dating people is that they are always together, stuck like postage stamps. Very different from when they were not dating, this time it was as if to show their loyalty, so they should not be separated. Even just because one of them is not willing to participate in an activity, then both of them automatically do not participate. Their activities and activities in an institution or church are reduced, as a result they are seen exclusively alone together. Actually, it's not good to be dating this model, it should be that those who are dating also mingle with other friends, not being alone. This is just advice, yes, but believe me, it won't hurt if you follow it.

Likes to hold

Touch/holding is also a sign of love, it's okay to hold hands, for example to help our partner cross the road or when walking together, meaning that what is being held is his hand. The problem is that if there is a gripping motion here and there, you know for yourself what it means. Negative things will arise, because of the sensitivity of certain body areas that will bring stimulation to someone so that he fails to defend himself against chastity during his courtship.

Madly jealous

A person if there is still jealousy, proves that he is still in love; because if he doesn't love, he really cares about that person. But if the jealousy is too late, it will be disastrous. Dating becomes a burden, there is no joy. Why is it said so? Because your life and movements are constantly monitored and suspected, talking to the opposite sex is wrong, receiving the call is also wrong, it's also not allowed to be brought home by friends, and what's more, the opposite sex glances at you. Wow, of course it is very painful to be in a blind jealousy courtship, even if you are not married, you are already suffering, especially when you get married, you will suffer for the rest of your life. In conclusion, free yourself from this suffering!

Often come home late

Surprisingly, people who are dating do not know the time. When in college or in a work situation, people feel that the days are very difficult to pass, but when they are dating, time passes without realizing it. That's why Sunday nights, which are said to be long nights, will feel very short. It's not uncommon if invites to watch his girlfriend, comes home late even until midnight. After that, just apologize to the girlfriend's parents. Not bad if you are forgiven, if you are scolded or insulted, of course problems will start to arise.

Like to fight

People also wonder about those who are intoxicated with romance, as we know sometimes they smile sweetly, but sometimes also cry. Why? Because usually those who make love are very sensitive, as smooth as silk thread, so they must really trust each other (trust each other), otherwise it can cause headaches. Fighting is actually normal, but if you fight every day, then you need to ask? Don't make your choice wrong. Your work will be chaotic, not concentrating, only taking care of the peace due to the quarrel. Very confusing.

Still other people's lyrics

People who are dating also face a lot of temptation, especially those who are dating long distance or long distance. Sometimes the communication is not smooth, especially when there is a time difference. That's why if they are in a long-distance relationship, if they can't stand the temptation, they will break up in the middle of the road. Why? Because when you're alone, there are glances here and there. If you're not careful, someone else will grab your boyfriend. As a result bite the finger. If the Chinese proverb says "Raise a chicken, become a bird", it flies to someone else's lap.

Spree

Prestige is a weakness that often occurs during courtship. Especially at times of struggle to attract the attention of his girlfriend. Many are willing to sacrifice to get it. Therefore, no matter how much it costs, whether it's eating out at a restaurant, sightseeing, gifts, or watching an expensive movie, it doesn't matter. Whereas previously that person was known to be very stingy, but dealing with his girlfriend and family he became Knock out (KO), turned out to be very royal. Later what happens, the credit card account becomes swollen, or the wallet looks like a hole.

Forget yourself

When dating someone can forget themselves, the world is thought to only belong to the two of them so they don't want to care about their surroundings, the important thing is that they enjoy the fun. The worst thing is that if the one who is dating does not realize that they are dating, they think that they are married. Forget yourself, its terrible!! Be careful, don't you forget yourself, right???

CHAPTER 8

PARENTS INTERFERENCE IN DATING

There are parents who do not want to know about their children's association, he said that today is the modern era, let the children determine their own future. This sentence may or may not be true, why? Because parents like this are considered parents today, who understand very well the living conditions of their children, but on the other hand, such parents are parents who are less responsible, because being a parent is a lifelong task.

Indeed, for young people who live with their parents, their dating activities are still monitored, even though your parents may be very busy, compared to those who study in the capital city and even abroad, they are all independent of their parents' monitoring, willing to do anything it's okay, and no one else is there. Which forbids. If you are with your parents, for example, you have to report to your parents and the time to go home has also been set, you can't go past 22.00 at night, for example, but those who live in a boarding house in the capital or abroad, want to head over and over, come home late at night, midnight or not. Home, no one cares. Just imagine, of course the risk is greater if there is no parental involvement at all.

I am sure that all parents love their children, they will not lead their children to wrong things or misery. Earlier, we mentioned earlier that people who fall in love are sometimes blinded by love, therefore it is the duty of parents to make them aware. Indeed, there are parents who have bad motivation, if their child's boyfriend is rich, then everything is not in question, it feels smooth like a toll road. However, if the boyfriend is poor (kere), he doesn't have a car, his motorbike is also worn out, now it's very difficult to get a permit for dating. There are many procedures. Sometimes because of this wealth problem, many parents are also blindfolded, so they take silly decisions, making the child miserable in their marriage. It turns out that wealth cannot guarantee happiness, On the other hand, the young people who are busy dating, have forgotten everything. Often he doesn't find the bad side of his partner, because the power of love is so strong, that whatever his girlfriend does is always good. Well, sometimes for this there is often a fight between the child and the parent. A boyfriend who likes to lie, is still being defended, its okay, for our pleasure, even parents are lied to, and it's okay. Just imagine, just in the courtship stage, the "prospective mother-in-law" even dared to be lied to, that's why don't be surprised if you get married, the wife will be lied to too, who's afraid! For men who are smokers and alcoholics and discotheques, if the woman who has fallen in love with him, is still fighting for it, it's okay to drink occasionally as long as she doesn't get drunk. Besides, what you drink is only beer which won't make you drunk. Well after marriage, what happened, you know.

I once heard the testimony of a mother of two, she said that when she was dating her husband had a bad character, apart from being a heavy smoker, he also often went to discotheques. Still lucky if gamble he does not like. However, after marriage or prostitution, the husband became increasingly violent, almost every Sunday night he went to drink and discotheque, at first the wife was invited, but because she already had children she was not invited again. Often comes home drunk and erratic, and likes to play hands hitting his wife. This happened time and time again, until finally the husband had WIL (Other Ideal Woman = mistress), then with courage and forced the wife to ask for a divorce, even though the two only sons had to be cared for by the husband, he did not question it anymore, he did not hold in honey. This is the result, because the eyes of people who are in love are blinded at that time. Parent's advice doesn't matter.

Once again we cannot ignore the

role of parents in terms of their children's courtship, although I do not agree that parents should impose their will on their children, because those who are dating are not parents and those who are going to get married are not them. It's really surprising, parents sometimes have instincts that exceed young children, and they seem to already know their future, although not everything is true, that's why their blessing as far as possible should not be ignored. Sometimes the choice and approval of the parents can be wrong, most likely because of the shrewdness of the girlfriend playing a play so that it tricked them.

There is a character in the Bible named Samson (Judges 14:1 - 4), at that time Samson saw a Philistine girl in Timma. Then he came home to tell this to his parents. This is good, because it turns out that Samson still respects his parents in terms of finding a partner. But what is regrettable is that he did not follow the advice of his parents.

Marriage is calculated by everyone in general is one time, although there are people who are many times, many times there must be something wrong. Because it's only once, it's necessary to choose and select the best, so the intervention of older people, especially our parents, is guaranteed not to harm. Excuse me ask? Have you been dating with the approval of your parents? Or is it still hidden? Those who are secretly, believe me, their joy and peace will surely be disturbed. Be patient, until they approve as long as our parents do not contradict God's word. Try not to ignore their interference in dating.

CHAPTER 9

LOVE DAY (VALENTINE)

It is said that there are two lovebirds, Armando and Monalisa, currently they are in love with each other, (must be with each other, so that it is not called one-sided) and have been dating until now for more than a year. It's not easy to get Monalisa, because Armando has to try quite hard, it turns out that other friends also want to take part. Right now they are always alone, if one is in church, then the other one is in Super Market, meaning the partner is also there. A day apart feels like a year. In the wallet, in the car, in the room, there is already a photo of the lover, just "sticky like a postage".

One day the two of them were in a park, in silence and intimacy accompanied by the sound of a sparrow whistling. Then the girl said that to the boy? May I ask a question? Oh, why not, my dear, just ask – you can ask a thousand questions. Then Monalisa said this, based on our knowledge so far, and with full awareness, if I were to ask, do you really and definitely love me? What do you say dear? Or is this still something to consider? What do you think the guy's answer will be? I'm sure the man will answer that he really loves. Then there is another second question, what will be the why do you love me? Guess what the answer is? I try to find an answer from the man, maybe he will say, because you love me, because you are beautiful, you are kind and so on. This is just my imaginary story.

We leave the two lovebirds above, we continue with the others first. In front of us, we said someone said love is blind, it's surprising that blind people can make love. Love (love). The word "love" (love) is the most important word in the English language – as well as in any other language, and it is the word that confuses people the most. Both spiritual and secular thinkers agree that love plays a major role in the life of a human being.

In the secular world, love is something of splendor that enlivens life, love makes the world go slow and love also makes the world go fast. Thousands and even millions of songs, books, magazines, and films are produced that are seasoned with love. I still remember when the romance film "Titanic" was screened in Indonesia, almost every day for more than a month the cinemas were packed with spectators, the queues were very long; many were disappointed because they ran out of tickets.

Below we want to see what is the background of people commemorating this Valentine's Day?

Why is February 14, Valentine's Day so important?

If we look further, there are actually two opinions regarding the history of Valentine's Day, namely; the first opinion says that Valentine's Day comes from the day of the celebration of Lupercalia. In ancient Rome, people worshiped the god Lupercus to take care of their livestock. So every February, the Romans held a feast to worship this god. One of the customs that is usually followed is to write a girl's name on a piece of paper and put it in a big jug. Then, each boy will take one name from the jug. The paired boys and girls will then continue to be together until next year's Valentine's Day.

Second opinion that, Valentine's Day originated from the reign of King Claudius. He thought that married men would be weak soldiers, so he forbade marriage in his territory. During the reign of King Claudius, there lived a Roman priest named Valentinus. He tried to go against the king's orders and secretly married a young couple who fell in love. In the end he was caught and imprisoned. After his death, Valentinus was later made a Saint. Although there are many versions of this event, in 496 Pope Gelasius established Valentine's Day as a day to commemorate Saint Valentine.

Symbols and Traditions on Valentine's Day

The most common symbol used on Valentine's Day is the heart. According to ancient beliefs, the heart is the source of all kinds of emotions. Then the heart is associated only with the emotion of love. Another symbol is a red rose. This red rose is believed to be the favorite flower of the goddess Venus, the Roman goddess of love. In addition, red is a color that symbolizes strong feelings. So, it has become a tradition on Valentine's Day people give red roses to loved ones.

Lace fabric is often used as a symbol of Valentine's Day. In the past, lace was usually used to make girl handkerchiefs. Hundreds of years ago, if a girl dropped her handkerchief, a boy would fetch it for her. Sometimes, if a girl sees an attractive guy, she will purposely drop her handkerchief. So then people will think about romance if they see lace.

So, at first Valentine's Day was a day of worship to the god Lupercus (version 1) or a memorial to Saint Valentine (version 2). However, along with the changing times, Valentine's Day then shifted into a day to express love to those closest to us in various ways, for example by giving roses, chocolates or a romantic dinner. As Valentine's Day approaches, shopping centers start to launch Valentine's Day products, restaurants and restaurants prepare special menus for romantic candle light dinners. Not to forget, television and radio stations broadcast special Valentine's Day programs.

What does the world say about love?

The word "l love you" is very popular, I'm sure everyone knows what it means. In Indonesian I Love you, lch Liebe

Dich (German), Wo Ai Ni (Mandarin), Kimi o ai shiteru! (Japan), Dangsinul Saranghee yo! (Korean) Te amo! (Spanish), Kulo Tresno kaleh Panjenengan (Javanese) and many more. Psychologists agree that the need for love is a primary need. For love, we want to climb high mountains, for love we want to cross the ocean, for love we want to cross the desert, for love we want to experience suffering. On the other hand, because of love, mountains become unclimbable, seas are not crossed, and suffering becomes life's misfortune.

Love makes flowers bloom, love makes a smile widen, love makes food delicious, love makes people sleep soundly, love makes people not stingy, love makes people eager to learn; but on the other hand love also makes flowers seem to wither, love makes tears flow, love makes it difficult to sleep, love makes grades in school bad,love make person difficult concentration work, love also which cause suicide. See, how shrewd and powerful love is.

If we agree that the word love or love is pervasive in human society, historically as well as today, we must also agree that it is the most confusing word. Notice, we use love in a thousand and one ways. We declare that: l love lce Cream, l love cats, l love my car, l love my house, l love my job, l love my wife, l love my book, l love my country and so on. We use love for things, for food, for animals, for countries, for books and for our fellow human beings, even for our God. If we haven't felt the confusion with this love, let's look at something else. When a man cheats on him, he says I love him, but the priest says it's a sin of adultery. The wife of an alcoholic continues married life with her husband after the drunken incident, the wife says this is love, but psychologists say it is addiction. Parents follow whatever their child wants, they call it affection, but family therapists say this is an irresponsible parent.

The love that the real world offers is temporary: When you are rich, I love you, when you are beautiful and handsome, I love you, when you are kind to me I love you. But when you are poor, Sayonara, when you are not beautiful anymore, Good bye my love, when you are mean to me then, Jai Jian (Goodbye in Mandarin)

People who are in love, have the concept that their lover has never done anything wrong. His mother could see the person's flaws, but the one who was in love saw nothing. His mother said: "Dear, have you considered carefully", then the one who was lulled said, "Mama, don't be suspicious, he is the only guy the best in the world." The power of love is so selfish, it makes the world feel as if it belongs to only two people.

When I was in third grade, I still remember the events of July 29, 1981, at that time the wedding day of Prince Charles of England to Princess Diana Spencer. News of wedding preparations and until the "D" day is always widely reported in both print and television media. Everyone was amazed by the beauty of Princess Diana, especially her face and hairstyle. In a fairly short time a lot of girls and some mothers at that time cut the hair of Princess Diana's model. Who is not amazed, a beautiful royal princess, but we see what happened to their love, it turns out that the love of this human child ends very tragically.

The dream of a person who is in love is a very perfect happiness, the image is that there is no quarrel at all, there is only love for each other. When they see another couple, full of problems, they say it won't happen to us. As time went on, a welcome greeting came to the world of marriage, it was not as imagined, sometimes debates occurred just because of small problems. Then our eyes begin to open, it turns out that our partner has the power to hurt us, he is sadistic too. Previously there was a concept that his girlfriend was the most beautiful in the world, but apparently there were also pimples. This is love in the world, the distance is actually close neighbors to hate.

What does God say about this Love?

When the world commemorates Valentine's Day, the words of love are scattered everywhere, from Super Markets, Newspaper Advertisements, and Television Advertisements to Trash Cans. Why do I say that? From the Super Market, we find flowers, Valentine's Cards, gifts, decorations with love, which will soon be thrown in the trash. True love should not be like that.

The love that God wants from us is love that is external and internal, meaning that when we practice acts of love, it is not only in our behavior, but also in our hearts. Actually when we talk about Love, we are faced with three different kinds of love, namely Philia love (Brotherhood), Eros love (Asmara) and Agape love (God). Love from God is unconditional love, unconditional love. Even if God is forced to put conditions, then the conditions are unconditional. Often we refer to love as

"Even though", not "because" "if" or "so. (Will be explained in another chapter)

See the difference between the love that the world offers and the love that God offers. When we say I love ice cream, it means that ice cream will be sacrificed, I will eat it. When you say I love that drink, then that drink will be sacrificed, I will drink; but the love of God is just the opposite, when God says he loves us, then He sacrifices Himself for us. See here the difference? To our girlfriends or partners, the spirit of love should take place every day, not on Valentine's Day as if they really love it, but usually they don't love each other.

CHAPTER 10

CALLING GIRLFRIENDS, ANSWERING MACHINE

Sorry, the boyfriend you called is not at home, but don't be afraid you can send him a message:

Press 1 to leave a message for him

Press 2 to make an appointment on a Sunday night Press 3 to invite a movie

Press 4 to ask for dinner Press 5 to talk to his parents Press 6 to leave a message to the maid

Press 7 to give a new message Press 8 to reveal a secret message Press 9 to stop talking

Press 0 to redial

How sophisticated is this idea? Is it true that the girlfriend is a company? Do you use an Answering Machine? Well, this is usually suffered by those who have a beautiful and attractive face because there are so many who have a crush on them. But there are some girls actually consider this as an advantage or pride. That's why the girl doesn't want to lose, she sells a little expensive. Instead of bothering to take calls here and there, it's better to just install an answering machine. The illustration above is just my imagination, I don't know if there has ever been a girl who practiced this or not? Can this condition occur? Maybe there is!

I try to imagine if I were the beautiful girl, then many guys had a crush on her, and tried to attract attention and hearts. Maybe the boys are of various types, some have rich parents' backgrounds, so they get splashed by being the son of a rich person. There are those who really struggle and then succeed in becoming rich people, so their status is cooler for rich young people. Others have tried their best and still haven't succeeded or have failed many times. And many other types..... Now they all want to attract the heart, as if in this world there are no other girls. So if the condition is like this, how do you behave as a girl?

From the answers I got through friends who joined my Friendster address, most of them said, if a girl is crush on by a lot of guys her name is hokey dong, don't reject it. Some of these other people have a lot of respect for boys, they say don't play with the guy, if there are a lot of crushes, choose one or the other, people who go out with just one person have enough headaches, is this really why you want to date a lot of people? After all, if you want to be a friend, that's a different story, just don't play with the guy, it's a girl, it won't be blessed by God. Trust me.

I do not know how your condition as a girl? Is it really a hooky position, many have a crush? But remember, after all a girl must choose only one suitable guy. Don't give too much hope to someone if we really don't really make that person a girlfriend. Unless you really want to work on him, but do you really lack work?

After all, one day a girl still wants to choose just one guy, once again it's impossible to buy all the boys. That's why there is a saying that "love doesn't always end in marriage." It means you can love many people, but marry one person. And when you're married, you have to stop loving other guys.

Then what about a guy who has many girlfriends? I don't know why this guy can have so many girlfriends? Did the Hong Kong Play Boy movie catch on or what? What is certain is that if a boy has many girlfriends, the girl loses. Society's assessment does seem to be one-sided, people usually turn a blind eye to a guy who has a lot of girlfriends, but if a girl looks like she has a lot of boyfriends, then if one by one they get bored and leave her, then the girl will have a hard time getting another guy, because there are negative image of the girl. This was said by a girlfriend in my Friendster, she admitted that she had dated four times, now she is engaged to her fifth boyfriend; and he admits that it is quite difficult to build stability with his girlfriend who is currently his fiancé. Many challenges and gossip and bad news were reported by people around who were not happy with him. His advice to fellow readers, try not to have many girlfriends, if close friends or friends want a lot, it's okay, so it doesn't happen again.

The experience he had. Have a lot of dizzy girlfriends, have to use the Answering Machine.

CHAPTER 11

TWENTY THREE REASONS GIRL DATES

If you are faced with the question of what is the reason for dating, of course the answers are different from one another. Some say the purpose of dating is to get married, some say it's just to fill their spare time, some say it's just for fun. Well, some of these answers are right or wrong, and can be dangerous, because we already know dating is not a fad or a game.

Some time ago I spoke to a girl on the phone, she said her sister was getting engaged. Then I asked, how about you, when? Why did his sister step over? Then he said, don't ask this question again, I'm bored, let's change the topic, if you don't want to change the topic, the phone will be hung up. Well, after I asked him why that was, then he honestly said that, too often when you meet people, especially his friends, let alone his parents, the questions are only about when to get married, which is his girlfriend and who is his girlfriend? Etc. He really wants to get married, he said, but the problem is that there is no one who wants to be married yet.

Below are 23 reasons why a woman is dating (if the answer is wrong, girls, don't protest?

1. Instead of hanging out in public to look for a partner, besides being not good in the eyes of your parents, you are also embarrassed by your parents, that's why you have to date.

2. Take care of yourself, because it's better to walk with a girlfriend than alone, because if someone naughty bothers them, they will think twice.

3. Save for saving, because usually when a girl is going out, the guy will always treat her, so the money can be saved.

4. Taxi fees are quite expensive, not to mention the tips that must be given, dating a girl will save on taxi costs,

because her boyfriend will pick her up for free, even take her home.

5. Parents like to worry about their daughters, especially when they are reaching the age of three, so that they don't worry all the time, a girl decides to date

6. Instead of crying there is no reason, then a girl is dating, so that the next time she cries, she can give a definite explanation that it's because of her boyfriend.

7. Dating is to maintain a beautiful appearance, why is that possible? Because a girl who is in a relationship, always tries to make the guy see her beautiful, so she must always put on makeup, even though she wasn't before.

8. Instead of being given the title of "antique" by people around and even by their own parents, it is better for a girl to make a decision to date

9. Dating is the same as activating a cell phone, rather than not using it on

Saturday-Sunday, so if you are dating, your phone will be used more.

10. Having a boyfriend is also a matter of pride, especially when you are hand in hand with a handsome guy.

11. Eliminate the laziness of getting up early, because your boyfriend is reluctant to find out if he is a girl who likes to sleep every day.

12. If by chance your car breaks down, there is still a girlfriend who voluntarily and freely pushes it from behind

13. Reducing air pollution, especially body odor (bb), because a woman who wants to meet her boyfriend must take a shower first and use powder and spray perfume.

14. Also to reduce bad breath, that's why it's very obvious that the girl is diligent in brushing her teeth, whereas before, sometimes she brushed sometimes not.

15. Dating also avoids the interference of mashers, because if a girl walks alone, the

boys are often stalked by her, but if the girl already has a boyfriend, she won't be bothered anymore.

16. Keeping things that you don't want to happen in the office, because as a secretary you are often tempted by the directors, but if you already have a girlfriend, it's a little safer.

17. To prove that a girl is an adult, because usually someone who is not yet an adult is definitely forbidden by her parents from dating.

18. Help increase the income of film producers, because girls who are dating are often taken by their girlfriends to see the cinema

19. Reducing the victims of the famine, because a girl who is reading a romance novel will usually forget to eat lunch and dinner, especially if she is dating herself, it's definitely not a problem if she doesn't eat for a day or two.

20. Dating also trains our feelings, sometimes

a girl has to cry because of the guy's actions, as well as sometimes laugh out loud

21. The girl is afraid of being accused of being a lesbian, or single, so then she starts dating, of course the one she is dating is a boy, not a girl

22. Because girls are the ribs of boys, at the time of Adam and Eve it was easy to know where they came from, because boys at that time it's the only one in the world, but nowadays guys are scattered here and there so it's a bit hard to find, this is why the girl is dating

23. Dating for a girl also increases interest in reading, the proof is that you are reading this book.

CHAPTER 12

PAIRSN ANDA BECOMES THE FIRST

Some people say, when dating please open your eyes wide, after marriage please close one eye, what does this sentence mean? This means that when dating, there is still the opportunity to change girlfriends if they don't match, but if after marriage, those who don't match must inevitably be matched, it's your own fault for not choosing carefully. In certain churches it is a rule that couples who take pre-marital counseling classes are not allowed to set a wedding day or book a restaurant for a party in advance, because if in the middle of the counseling lesson it turns out that they don't feel right, there is still a chance to cancel the marriage. What's the point, if the priest blesses a couple who fights constantly, it will be a lifetime of suffering.

A harmonious marriage couple does not mean that their household is free from quarrels, in fact there are people who say that fighting is a spice in the family, as long as it is not easy-going, it means not playing and hitting. That is why wisdom is needed to put the quarrel in the right circumstances. There is a colleague of mine recommends that when husband and wife fight, attention must be paid to focus on the context of the problem, do not interfere in things that are out of context, so be consistent on the topic For example, if the problem is problem A, don't bring up problem B, especially problem B, which happened three months ago. It means out of context. Sometimes just because of stagnant communication, misunderstanding, blind jealousy, has created a shocking reaction, this kind of thing must be wary of by male and female couples. I try to offer an acronym to describe a boy's love for a girl and vice versa. In short, make your partner the FIRST.

1. F = Faith

2. I = Initiative
3. R = Relationship
4. S = Sharing
5. T = Talking

F = Faith

This move is inevitable, too, because if someone is just trying to find a girlfriend, it will be quite difficult later. Moreover, we have already said that dating people is not a toy activity, because the risk is quite large, the evidence is that there are stress, severe depression and suicide because of dating. So, choose those who have faith, meaning those who fear God, and fear the same God. A man who has a God-fearing girlfriend will be safe, because he will be trusted even if they are separated for a long time. But that's not the goal, the most important thing is that if he truly believes in God, then all the problems in his life will have a way out, even if the process is not smooth.

I = Initiative

The initiative is important, because those who are dating are not dating statues, what they are facing is a living human who has thoughts and feelings. What is meant by initiative here is one with his partner always trying to be the best for his partner, loving each other? No need for cues or complaints, every need needed by the partner has been monitored long ago and always tries to help him equip and fulfill what is needed.

Just imagine if the boy and girl looked at each other, there must be no place to receive attention from the outside. But if one another without any initiative at all, of course they will get attention from the other, this is what is often the cause of hurt and slashed love, and the most important thing is that if there is a mistake it must be explained carefully, not with anger. Uncontrolled.

On the Tang dynasty; there was a

young man named Wang III. He is a stupid village youth. One day his wife asked Wang III to buy a comb. For fear of the husband forgetting so he pointed to the crescent-shaped moon in the sky and said "buy me a comb, but the shape must be the same as the moon."

A few days later, the full moon arrived. Wang III recalled what his wife had ordered. So he went to buy a mirror which is spherical in shape according to the shape of the moon.

When the wife saw the mirror, how shocked and jealous she was, then she ran back to her parents' house and said "My husband seems to have been playing badly with another woman." The mother-in-law looked in the mirror and with a sigh then said "He should have chosen a young woman! Why did he take this old and ugly woman?"

When someone feels that your partner lacks the initiative to pay attention to him, even now his attention is directed at someone else, it needs to be resolved with love, unlike

R = Relationship

Having a relationship is also very important in dating, because through this relationship, one can get to know each other more deeply. It's a bit difficult in the past when people dated long-distance, apart from being far apart, they didn't have a good relationship either. So you could say they didn't know each other. Well, those who don't know each other will then get married, and they live under one roof. Family background, education, character, nature, hobbies and so on are all different, so it's not surprising that there is a third world war at home, there are flying saucers and jumping glasses, meaning endless fights.

S = Sharing

The name of sharing demands an attitude of giving yourself and also listening to your partner, while living life together we should be sensitive to the pair. Besides that, it's also full understanding of understanding other people. At the time of our dating find are all good things, but when you are married ugliness that appear. Starting from the negative, untidy, less orderly, dirty and so on. That's why someone told us when

Sharing also means bearing each other's difficulties or problems, so that mutual understanding is created. We who come from families, different backgrounds, different traditions, if we want to be united will certainly cause various difficulties, for that we need mutual understanding, and mutual surrender; how wonderful it is to have such a partner.

4. T = Talking

Communicating with each other is also very important in male and female relationships. Life in a world that is so harsh that everyone is busy working, we often lose communication with one another others, because what happens is communication about business or work.

When just dating, maybe communicating via telephone for hours is not a problem, correspondence is long and myriad, but after get married it's not done again, because they are considered close and meet every day. Though with busyness, so meeting every day does not mean communication, but perhaps each of them took care of business while still paying attention to one another.

Failure in communication is characterized by frequent avoidance of communicating, for example, trauma when talking becomes a fight or hurt the heart, then those who are dating invites to watch movies, invites for walks and eats. So that finally they have been dating for years and can't get to know more about their partner. The problem will be big when they intend to get married, well at that time the depravity of each each will be exposed.

Actually, communication does not have to be through words, sometimes smiles, gestures, demonstrations and so on, including komunikai. A girl who when washing the dishes sounds like she's been slammed, we know she's emotional, so if she's aware of her emotions, she must quickly control herself. Use the given mind God to control our emotions, do not reverse it, so that emotions control our minds.

A husband who had just finished an argument with his wife decided not to greet each other. Early in the morning the husband had left for the office and now it was done without saying goodbye to his wife. At night after eating, he went straight to his room and went to sleep, as his husband did every day. Meanwhile, his wife also doesn't want to greet her husband, the important thing for him is that he has provide food for her husband, and that is enough One night, because the next day, the husband had to leave for the office early, so he quickly went to bed. But before that, he first wrote on a piece of paper one sentence that read "Mom, tomorrow morning at 05.00 wake me up..." Greetings Papa. Then he put it on the table and fell asleep.

The next morning, the husband woke up at 08.00, which means he was three hours late. He was very angry, because his wife did not wake him up. But when he got out of bed, he saw a piece of paper, but not what he wrote yesterday, but what his wife wrote sounds "Papa, pa wake up, now its 05.00, will you be late? Hello Mama. From the story above, we can learn a lesson that, prestige, has been fatal.

If we commit to make our partner the FIR-ST, then one does not need to insist on each other, imagine just f one another succumb to each other. If you have a boyfriend at this time, make sure he also reads this article, so there is balance, you don't just practice it alone, couple you also practice it. Once a song, make your partner the FIRST

Break up

Relationships between boys and girls that are built through introductions which are then continued with a more intimate stage which we call a romantic relationship or courtship, it turns out that not everything goes smoothly. Now, the relationship that has been fostered for maybe a year or two or even more can sometimes be destroyed in an instant and leave pieces of pain, hurt and heart slashed, followed by feelings of hatred, revenge and so on. That beautiful love suddenly turned into revenge and cruelty.

There are people who say that the distance between love and hate is only about one boundary line, which means it's very risky, like an "egg on the edge." Why did this breakup have to happen? There are several possibilities that I try to note below:

Dating long distance

Often the distance that separates one person from another becomes the problem of the dissolution of a couple who has been in love for a long time romance. Infrequent communication, minimal meetings lead to strained relationships. At first it had been built well, but due to being separated and the distance was far, the relationship began to feel bland, and over time there was no feeling of anything anymore.

Nowadays, it's okay, because the means of communication are so smooth and even sophisticated so that communication with foreign countries is not problematic. If 20 years ago communication difficulties were felt, then long distance relationships would be lost track.

Parent involvement

To this day, the involvement of

parents in their children's love or courtship issues has not been separated, even though often parents are always against the wishes of their children. Too dominant parents also often have a negative impact on the association and courtship of their children. Sometimes people also get confused, is it the child or the parent who wants to date? It is quite reasonable why parents do not approve of who their child chooses, as long as it makes sense then usually their children can comply.

However, they often overstep the boundaries, some are due to material and property problems, so that unwanted things often happen. There are many couples that I know, they have been dating for a long time, but because their parents didn't agree and they chose to obey their parents, they ended up breaking up. For those whose thoughts are mature, of course, it doesn't matter, they can get through this condition with common sense, but for those who are less mature sometimes it can have a fatal impact that continues with stress so they have to deal with the psychology department. It's still lucky if it's only a psychological limit, which is bad if someone tries to commit suicide.

Third person involvement

The involvement of a third person can usually occur because one of them is tempted or unfaithful to the other. This can happen most likely because of the estrangement of their relationship, busy work, lack of attention to each other, or like point 1 they were dating long distance. Sometimes they can't be blamed for one another, the temptation is quite a lot in their association, and there's also loneliness. That's why, which is somewhat guaranteed but not 100%, those who are dating should learn from each other and know themselves more deeply personally. If they only know each other for a month or two and then separate, then it is very possible for them to break up in the middle of the road.

Don't get along

For people who are dating, fighting is a normal thing because from there they can know and learn the character, character and nature of their partner. Indeed, there are almost perfect couples who never fight, but in this case we rarely find them. What's extraordinary is that every day we meet and fight, so sometimes it happens that the dating person cries every day. So, as a final decision, such a couple took a separate step. It's better that way, because if you're married then something like this is really bad, especially since religious teachings can't be divorced, then he will suffer to death because of marriage.

Characters that don't want to change

Sometimes character issues that don't want to be changed also become the struggles of couples who are dating can eventually cause them to break up if no one wants to change. Of course, this character problem is not trivial, but involves, for example, hitting, drinking, gambling, and drugs, which are thought to determine the future of the family. So as long as these addicts don't want to change themselves, it's probably difficult to continue their relationship. Indeed, if someone who has fallen in love, they don't care about this, but again, now many young people have started to think logically, so they don't want their family to be destroyed just because of this character and habit.

Actually there are many other causes that can lead to a person breaking up, but I think these 5 things are representative enough.

Now let's look at the consequences of someone who breaks up:

One of the risks of dating is breaking up, for those who have been dating for a long time and love is already very deep, of course the pain is also very deep. Not infrequently I find that due to a breakup there are people who are determined not to make love again. Thus his life is closed once with the opposite sex. This condition is still not so severe compared to some because of a breakup, he becomes heavily stressed, if the girl likes to smile alone, daydreams constantly, then makes up herself as beautiful as possible but is afraid to meet guys as well as the guy likes to look dapper, but kept hiding in the room, his behavior became very strange. And the most fatal, there are those who commit suicide due to a breakup, of course very terrible.

My advice, if you really don't get along with your boyfriend, and because of one thing or another you have to break up, let it be discussed properly. Isn't it time to start dating in a good way? Why if for those who have been in a relationship recently, breakups can still be considered normal, but it all depends on the person; so don't play with love. For those who love lightning, one breakup grows a thousand, but in reality sometimes one breaks up, it doesn't grow again. Think reasonable and logical, if you make love, don't let it be fatal, make love very happy, make love is also very dangerous. Psalm 34:19 says, “The Lord is near to those who are broken at heart, and he saves those who are crushed in spirit.”

CHAPTER 14

TRUE LOVENOT JUST JOB

When Prince Charles married Diana Spencer, wow television, newspapers, radio and magazines broadcast this news continuously long ago. There is a "great" pair of people about to get married, a handsome prince, beautiful women, what else is lacking?. The world is quite in an uproar with this news, many women follow Diana's hairstyle. However, there is something missing from them that we finally know that their marriage ended tragically, namely LOVE. True love is not just luxury, beauty, and wealth, but more than that.

Japanese crown prince Narohito's marriage to daughter Masako Owada June 9, 1993 also received enough attention from the mass media, both television and newspapers. What's interesting is, the wedding dress worn by the bride, is not just because of her elegance but also weighs 12 Kg. With clothes as heavy as that the bride is still smiling full of joy. Why is that? The most telling answer is because of "Love". The love of two human beings, has forgotten the weight of the clothes which is 12 Kg, although at this time we do not know how the state of the continuation of their love will be.

Too many people are selling the word "love" out, but how many people know what it means? How is true love? The Greek language has three expressions for the word "love"

Philia's Love (Friendship Love)

Andrew loves his wife, every day he comes home from work he always buys good food for his wife. The goal is to make his wife feel happy. So the "Love" that Andrew practices is Love with the emphasis "so". To be happy, buy good food, or for joy to buy new clothes or other souvenirs.

Eros Love (Romantic Love)

Susy really loves Roy because he is a handsome young man, they have been separated for a week, because Roy has a work assignment out of town, Susy misses him very much. Susy's love here refers to the emphasis "because", "because he is handsome, Susi loves him, so if one day Roy is not handsome anymore, we don't know whether Susy still loves Roy, maybe her love turns to Bob or something else.

Agape Love (God's Love)

Love that wants to give the best for others. It doesn't matter who it is, even if that person isn't love us. It is this love that we call the Love of God, the Love that "though." Love that does not demand conditions, loves because it is love, there are no frills. (Unconditional love). The love that even though that person hurts our hearts, has no strings attached.

Which model love do you have right now? I try to describe the three demands of love that must be owned by a human being, to be honest, in fact there is no true human love, only to the extent that the person lives; but we try to see the limits of our ability to true love.

TRUE LOVE NEEDS LOYALTY

Loyalty cannot be faked, it will run and be tested with time. Loyalty also doesn't require supervision, meaning a woman or a man doesn't have to specifically pay a security guard to spy on his girlfriend. Loyalty is only owned by people who really love, of course in the case of courtship, the loyalty needed only to one person cannot be more.

DR. Esther Lo Wu, a visiting lecturer when we taught, once said that there are three conditions that must be met when a man wants to propose to his daughter. First, he must love God. Besides loving God, he must also love his future wife, because what's the point of a person who loves God but doesn't love us. The third he must be "ABC", American Born Chinese Loyalty in true love even penetrates race, although usually parents often feel unhappy about this, but the most important thing is responsibility and loyalty. Ideally what is demanded by In general, in order to choose a boyfriend, choose one whose skin color is similar. But the reality on the ground is different, sometimes the environment is also very decisive.

TRUE LOVE NEEDS SACRIFICE

The concept of a person's sacrifice is usually very materialistic, meaning that when I sacrifice, I have to get something in return. No one wants to sacrifice and then get in vain. Likewise with a girlfriend, it should be from the existing sacrifices, the boyfriend must be loyal and still love, if there is no reward, then the courtship will break up. True love is not only when watching together, laughing, having fun, but at times of difficulty and experiencing difficulties.

II.LOVENEEDS ACCEPTANCE AS IS

Very perfect demands on their partner can also result in that dating becomes a pressure, even though we really hope that our boyfriend must be a good person, all of that has time. In other words, patience is needed, so that at this time we can accept our partners as they are.

A girl must hope that her boyfriend will be better than now, the change must be felt and real, and vice versa. When it comes to appearance (beauty), wealth is in the second or even third place or is not in question. What is important is acceptance as it is. Now if there is no loyalty to accept your partner as they are, of course it is difficult to continue this level of courtship towards marriage.

CHAPTER 15

LOVE TRIANGLE & THIRD PERSON

What is this love triangle? Is it a triangular shape? True love will be slashed and torn when a third person appears. Often this third person appears undetected. We don't know if we are ready to accept the third person. Maybe he was her high school friend? Maybe the neighbors too? Or maybe his ex-girlfriend? Maybe our parents too, now if they are our parents, the category is only limited to the third person, there are no attachments for love.

People who are dating often face various temptations and challenges, both from outside and inside. Sometimes we don't know what kind of challenges and temptations it will take. It could also be from the parents who do not approve of this relationship. The cause is unknown, but mostly due to economic problems. The difference in economic level that is quite striking also makes parents a barrier. Especially The claim is directed at the boys. The guy must be richer, or at least more educated.

Some time ago there was a guy who said to me, in terms of dating there is always injustice, then I asked why you said that? Then he said, the girls always choose the guys who are "ready to use" the term is called that. This means that the guy must have a degree, have a job, be rich, have a private car, if necessary have a private house and so on. Then I said, isn't it okay for a guy to sue too? This conversation stopped, because the phone credit ran out and was no longer continued. Then from the email I received, I just understood that apparently what is meant by "ready to use" is apparently the demands of most parents against their boys and their daughters. Sometimes the problem of love is ignored, so parents are sometimes the third person who gets in the way of their child's love.

Now if it's another love triangle, someone else appears who also loves the girl or the boy. I'm surprised, there are people who feel proud that many people love him, that's why even though he already has a girlfriend, and he still provides opportunities and hope for others. Sometimes what happens is that hope is too late, so it's as if the person has two girlfriends or more. His first girlfriend was not willing to let go, but he was also not willing to reject the second girlfriend, so finally a love triangle emerged. It is very painful, if it turns out that this problem is exposed, the victim will call him a love traitor.

Third, I asked a girl, how is her relationship with her boyfriend? He gracefully answered, don't mention it again? Then I asked why that is? Haven't you guys been dating for a long time, I've even heard that you guys are engaged? Then he began to tell a long story, "A year ago my boyfriend got an assignment "new in Jakarta, the company appointed him to be the Head of the Branch there. It was with a heavy heart that we parted ways, I was in Surabaya and he was in Jakarta. However, because of our busy lives, we rarely communicate, at least once a week every Sunday night via telephone, on weekdays sometimes via sms.

At first the communication was still smooth, but after three months I felt something had changed, often not answering the phone and replying to my text messages. That's why I secretly took a week's leave and followed it to Jakarta. I deliberately didn't tell him that I was going to Jakarta, I thought I would make a surprise on his birthday. I went by plane in the morning, then with Soekarno-Hatta Airport Taxi I went straight to his office which happened to be not so far from the airport.

Surprisingly it's already 10. am, he hasn't come to the office yet, I think his car broke down, got stuck or got sick. I purposely didn't introduce myself to his secretary, so he really didn't know I was coming. I waited for more than an hour, but what a bitch, suddenly I saw from the second floor to be precise in the parking lot, my lover got out of the car but was not alone, he was holding a woman with long hair who I finally knew she was one of the secretaries in the marketing field . I was devastated at that time, but I kept myself from getting emotional as if I had never seen it happen. The intention was to make a surprise for him, in fact I received the painful surprise.

That day he was really surprised by my presence in his office. After talking for a while, I asked the driver to take me to my aunt's house in Pluit area. That night we had a big fight, I do not accept this incident. While he was always defending himself, the reason was that there was an office task to be completed at the government office, which required hey are both present. But he thought I didn't see them getting out of the car and holding hands.

The next morning without telling him I went straight to the airport and returned to Surabaya. He repeatedly called me to apologize for the incident, meanwhile I had a hard time accepting it. How is that possible, because they are in the same office, while I am between Surabaya and Jakarta. After many times he apologized, I finally tried to accept him back. But it didn't last long, because just a week my friend in Jakarta saw him with the woman again at the Orchid Garden.

I tried calling his cellular, but he didn't pick up. Then I tried to call him with my friend's Celluler, finally someone picked it up, and the one who spoke was a woman. At that moment I almost fainted, but thank God it didn't happen. I tried to stay calm. I tried not to be angry, and held back tears. But I couldn't, my tears kept flowing. Three nights I couldn't sleep thinking about this incident, finally I still remember it was Monday morning, I happened to ask for sick leave to not come to work. I collect all the letters, gifts and including the ring in my hand. Then I packed it well, and through Express Delivery, I sent it to Jakarta. From that moment on I did not want to receive calls and news at all. To this day it's been eight months,

A love triangle, a love that can destroy humans. It's true that dating is fun, but if we break the rules of the game, there will be many victims. Victims of love can have bad consequences, some almost go crazy, some even accidentally kill their rivals and some commit suicide. Hi friends, if you are currently dating, be aware, be firm, be on guard; don't be influenced this vice. Do not try to give fresh air and hope to other people, if you already have a boyfriend so as not to invite trials and problems. Happy dating, dating is fun, but you are strictly forbidden to continue to be in a relationship, otherwise other tasks will be neglected.

CHAPTER 16

FUN TO LOVE!

It's clear that if we call it Fun Making Love, the connotation is negative, and the results are usually negative. Indeed, sometimes we are also confused, in modern times like this, there are people who don't have time to date because their work piles up, so it can be seen that there are people who are in their thirties and still have no intention of dating.

Many reasons were expressed when he arranged why they were still not dating. For guys, in general, they say they are not ready, do not have their own house. Jobs are still not permanent, salary is still not satisfactory, there are still responsibilities to parents. Meanwhile, for women in general they answered, they are more free to move if they are single, no one wants to go anywhere, if they have a boyfriend they are not free anymore; let alone meet the jealous.

Actually, for them, it doesn't matter if they don't have a boyfriend, but their parents are worried. That's why when we meet, apart from other topics of discussion, one of the topics that is always discussed is about marriage.

A few months ago there was a young woman who complained that we should call her Jenny, she said that Jenny was stressed when she called to Indonesia, especially when communicating with her parents. I asked why? He said, every time a call to Indonesia, parents always ask when to get married. Actually, it's not that Jenny doesn't want to get married, she said, the problem is that there are no people who want to marry me yet?

Ironically, I also often meet those who are still young and have been in a relationship. His parents paid a lot of money to get them to go to college, but not yet a semester he already had a girlfriend. Those who study abroad or who are far from their parents have full freedom of dating, parental supervision is very limited. Just imagine, what they want to do and do nothing that forbids it.

For young people who live with their parents, there are still "security or mines" to deal with. If you take your partner out, you still have to ask permission from your parents, then when you come home you don't dare to stay far at night. So, if they are in someone else's country or in a boarding house, of course, there is no one who forbids it. If you need to stay overnight, you don't need to go home again, no one forbids you and no one takes care of it!

Dating should be a positive means to encourage and strive to be more active in studying, but there are some of them who forget this, so because of dating the value has all fallen apart, that's why sometimes the food and boarding fees are used up.

Dating too early of course interferes with concentration in their studies, because dating itself is full of complicated problems. Therein lies everything, from love, smile, laugh, joy, happiness, to tears, anger, stress, jealousy, revenge, depression, almost suicide and so on.

Lessons on campus are already so complicated, plus the complexity of dating certainly interferes with learning activities more or less. Not to mention that those who are having fun dating then forget about their friends, and also God, so that nothing untoward has happened and they have to get married, even though they are still in their second year of college. Then of course they would have to leave college, and then the guy would have to find a job. Luckily if the parents have their own company, so this incident is still not so difficult to solve. But is this the future young people hope for? Of course not!

Whoever you are, boys or girls,

must be aware that our life is not just dating, because there are many tasks in this life that we must carry out. If you happen to be dating and then forget yourself, then you need to be vigilant. One of them must be sensitive to give a warning, so that this error is corrected, it is not easy but we have to do it. Hopefully!!

www.ingramcontent.com/pod-product-compliance
Lightning Source LLC
LaVergne TN
LVHW010610160826
845677LV00013B/3349

* 9 7 9 8 8 4 4 1 8 3 0 7 2 *